# OLD DANIEL

OR,

## MEMOIR OF A CONVERTED HINDOO

# OLD DANIEL

OR,

# MEMOIR OF A CONVERTED HINDOO,

WITH

## OBSERVATIONS ON MISSION WORK IN THE GOOBBE CIRCUIT

AND

## DESCRIPTION OF VILLAGE LIFE IN INDIA

**THOMAS HODSON**

GYAN

*Published by*

Gyan Publishing House
5, Ansari Road
Daryaganj, New Delhi-110002
Phone: 011-47034999, 9811692060
E-mail: books@gyanbooks.com

*Distribution Network*
gyanbooks.com
India, USA, Canada, UK, Australia



ISBN: 978-93-6780-145-1 (HB)

First Published, 1887

2nd Impression 2024

*Printed at:* Gyan Press, Delhi.



**OLD DANIEL**
Author: THOMAS HODSON

RIDDLE & COUCHMAN, LITH. 22, SOUTHWARK BRIDGE ROAD, S.E.

OLD DANIEL, SEATED IN HIS VERANDAH.

# 'OLD DANIEL;'

OR,

## Memoir of a Converted Hindoo,

WITH

## OBSERVATIONS ON MISSION WORK IN THE GOOBBE CIRCUIT,

AND

## DESCRIPTION OF VILLAGE LIFE IN INDIA.

*ILLUSTRATED WITH THIRTEEN ENGRAVINGS.*

BY

THOMAS HODSON,

*Wesleyan Missionary.*

---

WITH

INTRODUCTION BY THE REV. W. ARTHUR, M.A.

---

London:

WESLEYAN CONFERENCE OFFICE,

2, CASTLE-ST., CITY-ROAD;

SOLD AT 66, PATERNOSTER-ROW.

# PREFACE.

I CAN now, in my mind's eye, see Chickka, the washerman, as if I had met him yesterday; and I can see the mud houses of Singonahully, the mud wall of the village, and the temple of Runga, as if they were all before me. Yet five and thirty years are passed and gone since the afternoon when, in quest of medical aid, I rode past the village, hoping yet to see it the abode of many followers of Christ, not knowing that I was never to see it more. At that time Chickka was still a heathen. He was then between forty and fifty years of age, a greyheaded, resolute, self-controlled looking man.

At the mission-house of Goobbe we knew Chickka well. He was often present at our family prayer, but gave no signs of any religious conviction; and I cannot remember that he ever expressed more disapproval of idolatry than many did, who to this day have continued in their heathenism. Certainly I had no idea of the processes through which the mind of the washerman had passed. It would have been hard to conceive that one so ignorant and so simple, had as a boy, all untaught, seen as clearly the vanity of idols as well-instructed men could do, and had in his own simple way taken practical and striking steps to convince others of the justice of his views.

In the lifelike narrative of Mr. Hodson,—where every touch is that of one who has lived among the people, till their sayings and their doings, their surrounding scenes and modes of thought, are all familiar,—the reader will find a very curious light upon the processes of thought which, in the deepest night of paganism, may be passing in the mind of a labourer's lad who knows not a letter. We may feel assured that similar lights are shining in the darkest places now, and that millions of young minds are being prepared, as was the mind of Chickka, to turn from dumb idols to serve the living and the true God. Even were the incidents detailed in the following pages those only of the life of a single boy, they would be of great interest. But it is not as incidents that give interest to the story of an inward change of one mind, or of the outward windings of one life, but as a sign of what is going on in multitudes, and as a foretoken of the changes that are to come, that the highest interest attaches to such scenes as that of Chickka breaking the serpent-gods, turning the sword-gods into ploughshares, refusing to bow to the idol, or speaking lightly of the great god of the vicinity when his car was burned. Even the procession, which in all forms of idolatry, from that of India to that of Rome, forms an important instrument of public impression, failed to command the feelings of Chickka. How many men in countries where weeping Madonnas are exhibited have been tormented with the same curiosity which seized Chickka on seeing the tears streaming down the cheeks of Mari, the goddess of diseases! But seldom have courage and opportunity combined to carry the inquirer to a conclusion so decisive as that which rewarded the research of the poor washerman's son. I seem now as if I could trace the boy, in the struggling grey of the morning, down the gentle slope, till he reached the tank, found the spot where the idol had been cast into it, and, daring to break its head, laid bare all the mystery of the tears. That, too, was a step preparing him for the great change when he was to turn to One who is not the work of men's hands, but is the Maker of the mighty and the weak. And the same influences which prepared Chickka, and which eventually changed him into Daniel, are now at work in, I repeat it, millions of minds, where the influences are as much unseen and unsuspected as were at the time those of which the reader will find the account so striking.

Good Edward Hardey, whose words were the first that were sent home to the heart of the washerman with the power that quickens dry corns into sprouting seeds, and good Matthew Trevan Male, who baptized him as the firstfruits unto Christ in Goobbe, are both gone to their rest. Many others who have sowed on that field are also gone. Daniel has ended his course in peace. And still the harvest is not reaped. But the harvest is to come. In such a work delay, disappointment, and the deferring of hope are to be taken as but a call for more faith and more prayer. If the lights struggling in the heathen mind of Chickka were but an example of what is taking place in the minds of many, so also the change by which Chickka became Daniel, the steadfast Christian, was but an example of thousands of thousands that are yet to come. 'Behold, I make all things new,' says He who caused the light to shine out of darkness; and in the Mysore He will yet bring forth a new and glorious creation. In that country, at this present time, a terrible famine is making ravages. Even that calamity may be overruled for good. At all events it gives fresh emphasis to the call for all followers of Christ to enter in and work for God, where the harvest indeed is plenteous and the labourers are few. It may be that even in times of trial the Spirit will be poured out from on high, and that God will yet gladden with tidings of great joy the hearts of some to whom those fields are unutterably dear, and who have long waited for the full corn in the ear.

W. ARTHUR.

# LIST OF ENGRAVINGS.

# CONTENTS.

# 'OLD DANIEL;'

OR, A

# Memoir of a Converted Hindoo.

## I.

## DANIEL'S PARENTAGE.

BEFORE Daniel was baptised his name was *Chickka*, but we will call him Daniel from the beginning to the end of this little memoir. He lived sometimes at Goobbe, and sometimes at Singonahully. Goobbe is a large market town in the kingdom of Mysore, and Singonahully is a small village about two miles from Goobbe. The Wesleyan Mission premises are situated between these two places. If my young readers, for whom this little book is written, will take a large map of India, they will see 'Goobbe,' in Latitude 13° 19′ North, and Longitude 77° East. It is fifty-five miles north-west of Bangalore, and about seventy north-east of Seringapatam.

Many years ago,—it is not known exactly how many—a man of the Washerman caste left his native village and came to Singonahully. He brought his family with him, but left behind a box containing an idol and some other sacred things, in charge of the village priest. This man was Daniel's grandfather. In Singonahully he entered into friendly relations with the old village washerman, who was nearly blind, and helped him in his work. In due time one of the blind man's daughters was given in marriage to Daniel's father, whose name was Veera Chickka.

Daniel was born May 4th, 1799, or according to his own phraseology, 'I was born on the day Seringapatam was taken by the English.' It may here be observed that many of the middle and lower classes of the Hindoos do not keep any correct record of the time when their children are born, so that if no event of importance happens about that time, there is generally no means of ascertaining the age of any one in such families.

Daniel's father was always a poor man, so that his son was never sent to school; and he was never able either to read or to write; but, when quite a child, he manifested a very clear judgment in many things, and especially in the view he took as to the worship of idols.

## II.

## DANIEL'S FIRST PROTEST AGAINST IDOLATRY.

ONE day when Daniel was about ten years old, and living with his father in Goobbe, a relation of the family came from Toomcoor, on what, to him, was a very important matter; and he said to Daniel's father, 'Well, Veera Chickka, your father shut up our goddess in a box and left it, in his village, in care of the temple priest, and there she now remains. The goddess has had no worship paid her from that time to this; she is angry, and a great calamity has, in consequence, come upon me and my family. Come now, let us fetch the goddess from our ancestral home, and worship her here in this place.' The goddess referred to was Lakshmi, the wife of Vishnu, the goddess of wealth and prosperity. When little Daniel heard this proposal, it seemed foolishness to him, and at a favourable opening in the conversation he said to his relation, 'The goddess Lakshmi has blessed you with wealth, but she has left us in poverty; when she gives us prosperity we will worship her, but not till then.' Both Daniel's father and his visitor looked at the boy angrily, but said nothing; however, in the end his father decided not to fetch the idol.

The following is another proof of Daniel's decision; and it shows what a clear view he had of idolatry before he ever heard a word of Gospel truth. The account is given in his own words.

## III.

## SNAKE WORSHIP.

'When I was about eleven years old, my brothers and sisters were suffering from boils, and my parents asked a fortune-teller what they should do to get rid of them. He told my parents that the boils had come in consequence of their neglect of serpent-worship, and that the children would be cured if my parents would again worship snakes. These reptiles often take up their abode in white-ant-hills, after the ants have vacated them. My parents had been in the habit of worshipping serpents two or three times a year. Their custom was to pour milk, clarified butter, curds, &c., &c., into the holes of a white-ant-hill, when they knew there was a venemous serpent inside. The libations were accompanied by fastings, prayers, prostrations, and many ceremonial purifications. And now to remove the boils from their children they resolved to comply with the fortune-teller's directions, and go through a grand performance of serpent worship. They accordingly consecrated two old stone idols, made in the shape of serpents, and commenced the worship of them. I thought this was all foolishness, and before the whole of the ceremonies could be completed, watching my opportunity, I broke each snake-stone into two or three pieces, and threw them away as common stones. When my parents saw the broken images, and knew that it was I who had broken them, they were exceedingly angry, and my father said, with fury, "Son! is it proper to do so? Other gods may be false, but the Serpent-god is not. The children are suffering from the anger of the Serpent-god, and now you have broken his images, so that his wrath is increased; and what calamity will happen to us it is impossible to say."

'After my father was a little calm, I said to him, "Father, I believe that this worshiping snakes and their stone images is all nonsense. What connection can there be between boils on a human body and the image of a serpent? Have patience; no calamity will happen. Should any trouble come, we will then conclude that the serpent is a true god; and I will, in that case, get two other images made, and putting them in the place of the two broken ones, they shall be consecrated and receive regular worship." My father thought I was a strange child. However, in a few days, my brothers and sisters were quite well, and the belief of my parents in snake-worship died away.'

## IV.

### BIBLE IN THE CANARESE LANGUAGE.

DANIEL, at that time, had no teacher but the Holy Spirit. There were no Bibles in the

REV. W. ARTHUR'S CANARESE TEACHER.

Canarese language, which was the language spoken by Daniel; there were no Protestant Missionaries where he lived; no schools in which Hindoo children could be taught to read the Word of God; and no means whatever for acquiring a correct knowledge of the way to heaven. Had these means of salvation been in existence when Daniel was a boy, he would have been taught to worship the true God, and might have been instrumental in the conversion of many people. But his youth was spent in ignorance and in the service of Satan. Thank God, there is now a change for the better. There are Missionaries who preach the Gospel in many parts of the Mysore country; there are schools for children, and also for those converted young men who wish to be taught how to preach the Gospel to their own countrymen. The Scriptures are translated into the Canarese language, and may be had everywhere at a very cheap rate indeed. A copy of the Canarese Bible, printed at the Wesleyan Mission Press, in Bangalore, and beautifully bound, was presented, with Bibles in other oriental languages, to His Royal Highness the Prince of Wales, on his late visit to Madras.

This is a very different state of things from that which existed when Daniel was a boy. But there is very much yet to be done. The Missionaries have made a good beginning, but the work has to be completed; every man, woman, and child has to be converted; and therefore the young Missionary collectors all over England, have need to renew their efforts, that many more Missionaries may be sent to India every year.

## V.

### DIALOGUE BETWEEN A GENTLEMAN AND A SHEPHERD.

WE will now return to our history of the boy Daniel. In the same year that he broke the stone serpents, he played a trick on some impostors who were taking part in a religious procession, which the shepherds of Singonahully and the neighbourhood had got up. The shepherds in the Mysore country are very ignorant and very superstitious. This may partly be accounted for from the fact that they live with their flocks in the open fields daily, from morning to night, associate little with their fellow-men, and seem shut out from all means of instruction. A very learned Brahmin, who was at one time the Rev. William Arthur's Canarese teacher, wrote a number of 'Village Dialogues,' and in one of them the shepherd is most admirably described. The following extract is made in order to show the shepherd's ignorance, his creed, and his mode of worship. It is a fit introduction to the shepherds' procession which little Daniel interrupted. The extract is part of a supposed dialogue between an English gentleman passing through the country and a shepherd, whom he happens to see near the public road:

'The shepherd had a handkerchief round his head, a gray woollen blanket tied like a hood, and a six-cubit piece of cloth round his loins. Behind him came a flock of sheep, and behind the flock, in front, and on both sides there were barking dogs. The shepherd had a stick in his left hand, which he laid upon his left shoulder; in his right hand he had a long switch, and under the armpit a bag, in a small net of hemp-cord network; the net hung from the shoulder on the left side. Calling "Hus-si, hus-si, kiy-yo," to the sheep which were straggling on all four sides, he brought them together and drove them along; going sometimes before, and sometimes behind. Whilst he was going behind, he saw an English gentleman coming along in a travelling carriage, and said to himself, "Who in the world is this? A gentleman coming, as I'm alive! Why should I stay in his way? I'd better hide myself a bit." So he got behind a hedge, and fearing lest the sheep should stray, as he kept peeping and looking out every now and then, and huffing them with his cry, "Hus-si, hus-si," this gentleman saw him, and called out, "Ho Sir, *Gowda*,* come here." Hearing which, the shepherd said to himself, "What trouble has come now? He's calling me to come to him. If I go to him, I cannot tell what he may do to me. And if I don't go, I cannot tell what will happen. But they say that English gentlemen never do harm to anybody. Though I hear him, I'll just keep quiet as though I didn't hear, and if he calls again, I'll go." The gentleman, seeing the shepherd's great perplexity, and knowing that it

* *Gowda* is the head man of a village, and the word was used on this occasion respectfully.

GENTLEMAN AND SHEPHERD CONVERSING.

was through fear that he did not come, again called out, "Ho Sir, Gowda, Gowda, come here; don't be afraid; I won't do anything to you; you need not give me anything; come here, come and have a talk." On which the shepherd thinking within himself, "If I don't go to him after this, he may get angry, and I can't tell what he will do," delayed a little, as though driving his sheep; when the gentleman again called, "Come." "There is no getting out of it, I must go," said the shepherd to himself; and came near, and stood with the stick across his shoulders, holding the ends of the stick on both sides with his hands, swinging the switch that he held in his right hand, stooping, moving his head from side to side, and shuffling his feet. Seeing the shepherd, who thus came and stood, the gentleman entered into conversation with him, as follows:

*G.* "Well, Sir, *Gowda,* who are you?"

*S.* "I am a shepherd, my lord."

*G.* "What is your name?"

*S.* "My name is Bit-tare Shikkanu, Sir." (The words mean, 'If you let him go, you won't catch him again.')

*G.* "Bravo! If one let go your name, he

won't catch it again, eh? Well, what is your god's name?"

*S.* "Bír-ap-pa is our god, Sir."

*G.* "Bír-ap-pa, eh? what is he like?"

*S.* "That's good, Sir. What should god be like? It is in this temple."

*G.* "How do you worship your god? and how often?"

*S.* "We worship our god once a year, or once in two years, or if we miss that, once in three years. When the worship is made, there is a great gathering, numbers of people come—wind instruments, cymbals, tambourines, drums, flags, beggars, devotees, stoics, bearskin-capped shepherd-priests,—and as for brahmins, they are without number; they abound wherever you look. Besides these, shops, cocoa-nuts, plantain bunches, and bundles of betel leaves, innumerable. Mountebanks, ballad-singers, tumblers, companies of stage-players; all these, a great gathering, Sir. Then worshipping god, presenting flowers, lighted wave offerings, offerings of money, of ornaments, votive offerings, and consecrated cattle; persons who give their hair, cocoa-nut scramblers, lamp bearers, offerers of fruit and flowers,—many people come together, and we worship our god *Bír-ap-pa.*"

*G.* "Is the temple, where your god is, very clean?"

*S.* "Yes, Sir. If god's place is not clean, what is? God is set up in a stone temple. Once a year, or once in six months, if we open the door we open it; if we don't, we don't. Nobody goes there at all except at the feast. If a temple like this is not clean, what is, Sir?"

*G.* "But don't you sweep the floor and sprinkle it with water every day?"

*S.* "Who is to sweep it every day, eh? Once in six months, once in three months, or once a year, the priest opens the door, and if there be a feast or full moon, he sprinkles and sweeps a little, colours and whitewashes the walls with red earth and with white earth, streaks them, brings mango leaves and makes them into festoons over the door; and if we worship and bring flowers, we do; and if we don't, we don't. Such a god is our god, Sir."

*G.* "Bravo! a very fine god indeed! But what do you do to this god at the feast? Tell us a bit, and let us hear."

*S.* "What can I tell you, Sir? We are

silly shepherds; all our language seems queer to you."

*G.* "Never mind, tell me, *Gowda.*"

*S.* "Well, Sir, eight days before the feast, the priest must get his head shaved, bathe himself in water, and take but one meal a-day. Having thus taken but one meal a-day for eight days, he, on the feast-day worships the god in the temple, praises it, prostrates himself, and begs it to do us all good. He then comes out and kneels in the court of the temple, near a stone pillar in front of the god. He shuts his eyes, and rests on his hands and knees. When he has taken this position, all who have come to the festival to worship our god *Bír-ap-pa*, bring cocoa-nuts. and going up to the pillar where the priest is kneeling, they take the cocoa-nuts in their hands, and press upon one another, each crying, "I am first, I am first." Then ten of the most respectable people come out, stand apart from the rest, make the people who are pressing forward stand back, and take the cocoa-nuts, which the people have brought, into their own hands. Four others, strong men, stand near the priest; the elders hand the cocoa-nuts to them; and they keep on breaking them on the priest's head; the priest, all the time, having his eyes shut, is down on his hands and knees before *Bír-ap-pa*, holding out his shaven head, until great heaps of cocoa-nut fragments are piled up as high as an elephant on both sides of him. And though so many nuts are dashed against his bare skull, the priest feels no pain, and never utters a sound which indicates suffering. Such a glorious god is our god, Sir. No matter what trouble threatens he wards it off. He always takes care of us."

*G.* "How is it, master shepherd, that you do such a silly thing as this? There is a trick in breaking the cocoa-nuts on the head of the priest. The people who break the cocoa-nuts are clever jugglers. They have a store of cocoa-nuts which have been previously broken and stuck together again. They substitute one for the other, and so deceive the people."

*S.* "How it is, Sir, I don't know. You are a gentleman and you understand it. I only say what everybody says, Sir."'

The above dialogue shows a shepherd's creed, his ignorance, and his mode of worship. And it was a festival, a procession, and worship such as this that the shepherds of Singonahully were celebrating when Daniel interfered. The following is his own account.

## VI.

### THE CRY OF 'SNAKES! SNAKES!'

'After some of the ceremonies had been performed in honour of the shepherds' god, *Bír-ap-pa*, certain consecrated things were carried by the priest, and others by his wife, to a particular tank, or artificial lake, where special washings and other purifying ceremonies had to be performed. The shepherds and their relations were accompanied by musicians, dancing-girls, religious beggars, and many others. They also had a Brahman to perform the appointed purifying ceremonies at the tank. These being completed the procession came back with great pomp. The priest, his wife, the hired Brahman, and some others, walked on garments which had been spread in the way on purpose for them to walk on. As the wife of the priest came along carrying a *Kalasha*, a particular kind of water vessel, which for the time, with its contents, was

AN IDOL PROCESSION INTERRUPTED.

held to be pure and sacred, she pretended to be under the influence of some god. She began to swing and roll herself about in a most strange manner, trying to make the multitude believe that *Bír-ap-pa*, or some other god or goddess, had entered into her. She struck and kicked those persons who tried to hold her, and abused many in very foul language. I saw and heard all this, and thought the woman was a great hypocrite. I could not believe it possible that any god or goddess would compel a woman to act in such a foolish way. I said to myself, "What a shameful impostor this woman is!" After thinking a little as to what I could do in order to expose her, and shew the people that she was deceiving them, I watched for a favourable opportunity, and then cried out, "Snakes! snakes!" as loud as I could. This produced immediate confusion. The priest and his wife, through fear of being stung by the snakes, tried to get away; no one knew which way to run; some were knocked down, and the sacred things which the priest and his wife were carrying fell to the ground and were broken. The worshippers of Bír-ap-pa, and the mob of followers all dispersed in vexation and grief; but I went home greatly amused.'

## VII.

### SWORDS BEATEN INTO PLOUGHSHARES.

In the second chapter of Isaiah, and the fourth verse, we read, 'They shall beat their swords into ploughshares;' and by the context we know that these words are part of a description of that universal peace which will follow the preaching of the Gospel in every part of the world. This beautiful poetic image made use of by the prophet Isaiah, has been adopted by many writers ancient and modern, and the words are often quoted by eloquent public speakers, when referring to millennial times; but it is probable that none of them ever expected to hear of the words being literally fulfilled. This, however, was accomplished in Singonahully by our little friend Daniel. We have seen that Daniel's heathen name was 'Chickka,' and his father's name was 'Veera Chickka,' that is *hero* Chickka; but whether any deeds of heroism were ever displayed, either by Daniel's father or by any of his ancestors, is not upon record.

However, we do know that when his old grandfather left his native town and came to live at Goobbe, though he did not bring the image of the family goddess with him, he did bring some old swords which had been in the family very many years. These swords had often been worshipped by Daniel's forefathers. We may here observe, in passing, that all Hindoo mechanics and other workpeople regularly worship their tools and other instruments by which they gain their living. They put up any of their implements as representations of *Vishwa Karma*, the architect and artificer of the gods, (*Vishwa* means the World or the Universe, and *Karma* means Work) and pray to these tools for success in business, war, agriculture, etc. Thus a carpenter places a hammer or a saw before him, and putting both his hands to his forehead bows to the instrument, and asks for its help in the work to be done. The barber worships his razor; the blacksmith worships his bellows; and the farmer his plough, oxen, etc., etc. Daniel's forefathers having worshipped these old swords, Veera Chickka continued the time-honoured custom. On a special occasion he invited his relatives and friends to come and join in the worship, and in the feast which always followed it. This happened when Daniel was about thirteen or fourteen years of age. Preparatory to the worship, his parents cleaned the rusty swords, decorated them with flowers, and placed them upright against a wall. When the proper time came, they and their visitors made offerings to the swords, of plantains, cocoa-nuts, rice, etc. After this, they burned incense to their ancestors who were the original owners of the swords, and then falling prostrate before them they all cried out, 'O, our gods, prosper us: O, our gods, defend us.' After the worship was over, all the visitors partook of the feast prepared, passed the evening pleasantly in conversation, and the next morning returned to their own homes. Daniel says, 'I was much impressed with the foolishness of all these proceedings, and I said to myself, "What benefit can be derived from the worshipping of these old swords? I am determined to put a stop to this in some way."' He thought the matter over several days, and by that time his plan was formed. So one day, when no one saw him, he took the swords, with the box in which they had been carefully placed, and started for the blacksmith's shop. But on the way he met his brother, who stopped him, and the following altercation ensued, as given in Daniel's own words: '"What is that you have got in the box? and where are you going with it?" said my brother. I replied, "O, nothing particular." But he would not allow me to proceed without his looking into the box and having a plain answer to his question. I therefore said, "Brother, as our people have been accustomed to worship these old swords, I think they had better be made into some proper shape. I am therefore taking them to the blacksmith, that he may put them into his fire and make an idol of them." My brother, on hearing this, was quite shocked, and said, "Do you mean to say that you are going to break up these sacred relics, which have been handed down to us from our heroic forefathers? I think you are mad. I will go immediately to our father and tell him what you are doing." So saying he went home in great anger, and I went on to the blacksmith. When I arrived at his shop, I found several men outside waiting to get something done to their agricultural implements, and they all looked at me very enquiringly. I said nothing, but put down my box of swords, and sat upon it. At length the blacksmith said: "Well, Chickka, what have you come for? What have you got in that box?" I opened the box and shewed him the swords. On seeing them he said, "What have you brought these things here for?" I replied, "These old swords have been occasionally worshipped as gods in our family; but I don't see that any benefit can be obtained by worshipping such things; in their present shape they are useless; I think they may be made into something useful. I have therefore brought them here for you to make ploughshares of them." As soon as I had uttered these words, all the farmers present seemed terrified, and one man exclaimed, "If you do this, your family will never prosper; these are gods." I said, "Very well, we will see whether they are gods or not, we will give them a fair trial. We will put them into the fire, and if they are gods they will jump out: and if they are not gods they will melt like common iron: let us see." The blacksmith did what I wished. He made one ploughshare immediately, and the others afterwards. The lookers-on said

BEATING SWORDS INTO PLOUGHSHARES.

nothing, but they doubtless expected some dreadful calamity would happen to me. When my father heard what I had done, he was very angry, and said, "This boy is born to destroy our gods and customs." For several days he would not allow me to enter his house: but in two or three weeks my father's displeasure passed away, and the matter of the swords was not mentioned again. But all the members of our family complained that I never bowed to the idol when I passed the temple as they and all the other people in the village did. To this, when questioned, I had only one answer, namely, "I don't believe that any image made by human hands can be God."' This boy was evidently taught of God, without the aid of any human means. He could not read; the example of his parents and friends was bad, very bad; and he had never heard one word of Gospel Truth.

Every one who has seen an English plough will know that a few old swords would not supply material for one English ploughshare, but an Indian plough is a very different thing, and is well represented by the accompanying sketch. All the iron required is a little bit at the point which enters the ground. The plough is very light, and may easily be carried by a *boy* from the farmer's house to his field

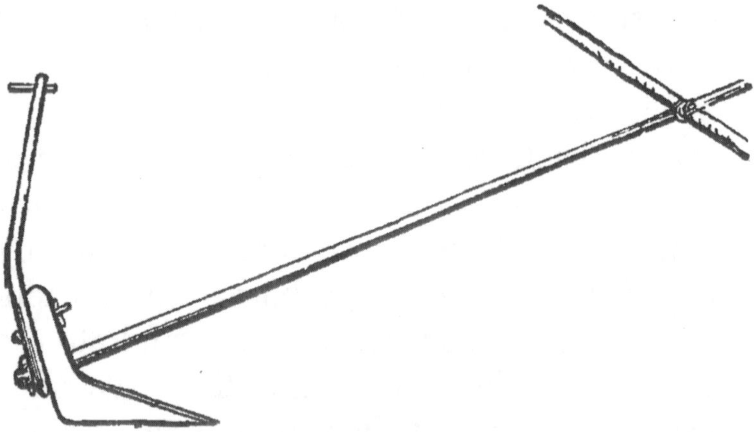

AN INDIAN PLOUGH.

in the morning, and back again in the evening. A *man* may be often seen carrying *two* ploughs, one on each shoulder.

## VIII.

## INDIAN AGRICULTURE.

WE may imagine that the first plough ever used in India was a crooked branch of a tree; and we may also imagine that when a suitable branch could not be found, the skill

A MYSORE MAN PLOUGHING.

of the best mechanic in the locality was called into exercise to make something that would do as well as a crooked branch. Then, in the course of years, some original genius improved upon nature by adding, when needed, a harder substance than wood; and hence the bit of iron now added to form the Indian ploughshare. Beyond this the farmer who lived a thousand years since in the Mysore country did not venture to go; and the present race of cultivators, relying with implicit confidence on the wisdom of the ancients, look with suspicion on all proposed improvements. This primitive instrument, represented in the engraving, having been tied to a bar of wood laid across the neck of two bullocks, and placed under the management of a ploughboy, the ground is scratched a few inches deep after every shower. This process prepares the ground for the seed, and nature being generous, a very fair crop is produced. In the Mysore country the farmers were never so prosperous as they are at the present day. Thanks to English authority, the people are not oppressed as they were under the despotic rule of their own native princes. The Government is the great landlord; the rent of ground has not been very much increased; the taxes have been reduced, and the produce of the soil fetches three times the price it did forty years ago.

## IX.

### HOW A SCHOOLMASTER BECAME A GOD.

WE have seen how some old swords were worshipped by Daniel's parents and friends, and we will now show how, many years ago, a god was made out of an old schoolmaster, and is worshipped at the present day. The legend is that, about two hundred years ago, there lived in Goobbe a very efficient schoolmaster, who was celebrated all over that part of the country for his learning, wisdom, and sanctity. He lived to a good old age, and then died. The respect in which he had been held during his life was manifested at his funeral, when there was a very large gathering of mourners. His death was looked upon as a public calamity. But he would doubtless soon have been forgotten had it not been for the gratitude and activity of one of his pupils, named Burree Gowda. This man had, during the course of twenty or thirty years, become very rich, and a person of considerable influence. He attributed all his success in life to the teaching and good example of his old schoolmaster, and he felt disposed to do something to perpetuate his memory. He therefore one day called together all the influential men of Goobbe, amongst whom there were probably a few of Burree Gowda's fellow-students, and to this assembly he opened his mind fully. He enumerated the excellencies of his old teacher, and stated his conviction that the good schoolmaster was something more than an ordinary mortal; indeed, that he was an incarnation of some deity; adding that, being divine, he ought to be worshipped. To this opinion the assembly assented. He next proposed that a temple should be erected, and all arrangements secured for the schoolmaster being worshipped as the god 'Goobbe-appa'—that is, Goobbe-father. All agreed to this also, as being calculated to benefit the people of Goobbe, as well as to do honour to the schoolmaster. But when Burree Gowda proposed to meet all the expenses himself, we may fairly conclude that the proposal was carried by acclamation.

In due time the temple was built, an idol (the bust of a man with a face of gold) was made, and, with the usual ceremonies, '*Prâna pratishta*' was performed. This is a special ceremony, by which the Hindoos think life is imparted to an image, or that a god is made to enter into an idol. Thus they supposed that the deified old schoolmaster entered into the image of 'Goobbe Appa,' which had been made for him to dwell in. And there, in that temple, he is the most popular god of all within twenty or thirty miles of Goobbe. He is not only worshipped daily by many who live in the town, but also once a year by eight or ten thousands of people who, at the anniversary, come in from all the adjacent towns and villages.

When Daniel was about fourteen or fifteen years of age, he had to take part in one of these annual festivals. It appears that some rich man, probably a descendant of Burree Gowda, had determined that year to have a specially grand procession. He, therefore, months before the time, began to make preparations. He had a car, or carriage, made, purchased fireworks, lamps, torches, etc. The washermen far and near were told to bring cloths of different colours with which to cover and decorate the car, and payment for them was promised. Some people brought garlands of flowers, evergreens and other foliage as presents; so that when the procession started at midnight, with thousands of lamps and hundreds of torches burning, the vast crowds of people gazed with wonder and delight. Daniel had to attend and help to decorate the car with such cloths as his father had been called upon to supply. This being done, he had to carry a torch. The procession had not proceeded very far before some of the cloths on the car took fire, either from the lamps or from the fireworks, and a terrible confusion was immediately produced. The priest of the temple, who was riding upon the car, was very severely burned, while shrieks and cries were heard on every hand from many who had been knocked down and injured. When the priest was helped out of the burning car he ran into some deep water to cool himself. The idol also was taken out of the flames, and finished its journey in a palankeen. Daniel says, 'I saw all this: and at the time when the priest came out of the water, he ordered me to walk by his side, and light the way for him with the torch which I had been directed to carry; but as I proceeded, a sharp thorn ran into my foot, and gave me great pain, so that I could not walk, but was obliged to sit down. The priest commanded me to get up, and come along with him. I said, "Be patient, my lord; I am suffering from a thorn in my foot." However, in a very loud and angry tone he said, "Get up, I command you, and come with me after the god." Then I felt angry too, and replied, "Why do you bawl out in that way? The god does not want me; but if he does, I cannot come; I am lame; he may help himself." On hearing these words of contempt for the god, the priest abused me very much, took the torch from me, and ordering another person to carry it, he left me on the ground trying to get the thorn out of my foot. Whilst I was lying there in great pain, I heard a cry of "Thieves! thieves!—robbers! thieves!" and saw many men running back from the burning car to the town. I learned afterwards that a great many robbers had laid their plans to enter the town quietly as soon as the inhabitants had left their houses and

MISSIONARY PREACHING NEAR ENTRANCE TO GOOBBE.

shops to join the *Goobbe Appa* procession. The thieves did not accomplish all they planned to do, but they stole very much valuable property.' All that happened at this festival served to convince Daniel that 'Goobbe Appa' was as helpless as any other idol, and that the so-called worship was senseless.

This whole account of 'Goobbe Appa' shows how Hindoo ideas as to God and His worship differ from the ideas of Christians who have been favoured with the Holy Scriptures. And the account will, it is hoped, excite pity for the Hindoo men, women and children; and induce the juvenile collectors, as well as others, to renewed efforts for sending more Missionaries to India.

At the annual festival, which lasts ten days, the Missionaries are fully engaged distributing tracts, preaching, and conversing with serious inquirers who have come from distant towns and villages. The accompanying sketch, in which a Missionary is preaching, was taken near the entrance to the town of Goobbe, close to the 'Mantapa' in front of 'Goobbe Appa's' temple. A mantapa is an open temple, or halting-place for an idol on procession days.

## X.

### THE IDOL WHICH SHED TEARS.

WHEN Daniel was about sixteen years of age, the cholera broke out for the first time in Goobbe. It prevailed for about eighteen months, and many persons died of it every day. The inhabitants of Singonahully, and of all the other villages round about, were in consequence very much afraid to enter the town. One day, during the prevalence of this disease, an ass belonging to Daniel's father was missing. It had strayed, and Daniel went from Singonahully towards Goobbe in search of it, but without any intention of entering the town. On his way he met a great crowd of people. There was in the crowd something different from anything of the kind he had ever seen. He noticed that many of the people had their bodies painted yellow, and there was to him something very strange in their appearance, dress, and conduct. As he was gazing at the people and walking slowly along, he stumbled, and fell over a dead body, probably a victim of the cholera. He was very much alarmed;

and as he got up from the ground in agitation and terror, he saw his uncle coming towards him, who, thinking Daniel was going into the town of Goobbe, threatened to beat him, and said, in a very angry tone, 'Why are you going to that cursed place?' To escape his uncle, Daniel run into the thickest part of the crowd, and he then determined to go along with them, and see what was to be done. As they proceeded slowly towards the large tank, (lake,) he saw that a few men near the front were carrying an image of clay in the shape of a woman. She had been worshipped to avert cholera, and now the worshippers were taking the idol to throw it into the tank, as the last act of their devotional ceremony. Daniel was a close observer of all that was done, and he saw at one time, when those who carried the idol held it up higher than the heads of the people, tears run out of its eyes. Many persons in the crowd saw the tears, and they all fell prostrate before the image of clay, and cried aloud, 'O mother, why are you shedding tears? Tell us what grieves you, and we will do whatever you require.' The priest, immediately pretending that the goddess had entered into him, commanded, as if the idol spake, that more sacrifices should be offered. On hearing this, all the people stood still. They did not go on towards the tank, but re-remained just where they were, until the animals could be brought for the chucklers to offer them in sacrifice. The *chucklers* are the lowest class of persons in India, and to Europeans it is unaccountable that, under any circumstances, they should be called upon to act as priests. But so it is, in some localities. They sacrifice to M ri, as the goddess who sends and takes away cholera and all epidemic diseases. There is good ground for the opinion that these outcasts are the descendants of the original inhabitants of the country, and that they have been subjected to degradation by a succession of conquerors. Their invaders found them with a creed, and certain customs to avert diseases, with which they have never interfered. Hence the present practice. After the Goobbe procession had waited a long time, fifteen buffaloes and a few sheep were brought and sacrificed near the idol. This having been done, the weeping goddess was satisfied, as shown by her shedding no more tears. The people took this as a very favourable indication that the cholera would cease from that moment. They proceeded to the tank, threw the idol into it, and returned to their homes rejoicing. Daniel, who had witnessed all these proceedings, had his curiosity excited, and thought there must be some deception in the matter of the idol shedding tears. And in this sceptical mood he went home to Singonahully perplexed, but resolving to get at the truth if possible. The idol had not been thrown into deep water, and he determined to rise early next morning, go to the tank, and examine the head and eyes of the idol. He did so, and the following is his own account: 'Before daybreak I ran from my father's house to the place where I had seen the idol thrown into the water, and I found it, just as it had been left the previous evening. I saw many plantains, cocoa-nuts, and other things, which had been offered to the idol, scattered about on the ground. Such as were not spoiled, I collected in order to take them home with me. Having done this, I commenced my examination of the image. I broke its head, and the whole mystery was revealed at once. I found in the head an earthen vessel, round as a ball, with two small holes in it; these corresponded with the eyes of the image; and I perceived that when the vessel had a good quantity of water in it, if those who carried the image made it lean forward a little, a small quantity of water would ooze out of these holes, and trickle down the face of the image like tears. I rejoiced greatly that I had found out the trick by which the people had been deceived; and, chuckling, I took up the fruit which I had collected, and went back to Singonahully without any one knowing what I had done. I was afraid to take my load of cocoa-nuts and plantains to my father's house, lest I should be questioned as to where I had been and what I had done; so I hid all my booty in a hollow banyan tree outside the village, and resorted to this store-house whenever I wanted a treat. However, when my young friends and others saw that every day I had an abundance of good things to eat, they were desirous of knowing where I got them. After a little delay, I told one of my young friends, not only where I obtained the fruit, but also all that I had done with the idol. He was terrified; and running into the village, he published the whole affair. The villagers were alarmed; they feared some dreadful result, and wondered at my wickedness. From Singonahully the news was soon carried to Goobbe, and I was summoned to appear before the chief magistrate of the town. He heard all that my accusers had to say, which I admitted to be true. He was very angry, and said to me, "On account of your wickedness, the cholera has not been removed yet, and as a punishment you must be imprisoned for a long time." I was immediately sent to the jail; but after I had been confined there two or three days, I had an opportunity of speaking to the magistrate; and I then told him how the people had been deceived, and cheated out of their sheep and buffaloes, and how I had discovered the trick when I broke the head of the idol. He was evidently annoyed, either at the deception practised on the people or at the fact being discovered; and after a few minutes' hesitation, he released me from prison.'

## XI.

## DANIEL IN TROUBLE.

About that time Daniel's mother became insane, and her friends were all of opinion that she was possessed of an evil spirit. This troubled Daniel, for he loved his mother very much. The remedy for such cases was prescribed, and the foolish ceremonies were duly performed by Daniel's father. After several months the poor woman recovered, and it was supposed by all the friends and neighbours that her cure was produced by the ceremonies, charms, and incantations which had been made. It does not appear that Daniel raised any objections to the performance of these superstitious ceremonies, or, on the other hand, that he had any faith in their efficacy; but he rejoiced greatly when his mother was restored to soundness of mind. Daniel says: 'When I was about nineteen years of age, I gave myself up to many wicked practices, and my conduct for many months was very immoral. Our family was poor, and I determined to leave Singonahully for some place where I might get on a little better in the world. But one of my uncles, who was a wealthy man, interposed, and took me to his house. He set me to work in his fields, and assist him generally in agricultural operations. Whilst so employed, I wished to be married, but met with two difficulties: the first was poverty. My father had no money; and as the marriage ceremonies and feasts are always expensive, I knew not what to do. Then there was another hindrance: the father of my intended wife withdrew the consent he had formerly given to the marriage, on account of my conduct in connection with the cholera goddess. But my generous uncle interposed, and induced him to give his consent. And then he removed the other difficulty by paying all the marriage expenses himself. With this uncle we lived many years in Goobbe; and when he became an old man, I managed his farm for him, and at the same time I carried on my work as village washerman.'

## XII.

### THE FIRST SERMON PREACHED IN GOOBBE.

On the 1st of September, 1836, Goobbe received the first visit of a Protestant Missionary. The following is an extract from Mr. Hodson's Journal: 'After spending a few days with Captain (now General) Dobbs at Toomcoor, I rode over to Goobbe, a distance of twelve miles. When I had arrived within about a mile of the town, I was met by a number of the principal inhabitants, who expected Captain Dobbs. On finding out their mistake, they politely paid me the compliments intended for their local governor. They accompanied me to the "gate of the city," and their trumpeter gave notice to the whole town that "a person of distinction" had arrived, and it was very soon known to every one who loved to hear news that the visitor was a Missionary. After breakfast, which Captain Dobbs' servant had prepared for me, I went into some of the principal streets of Goobbe to make my observations on the suitability of the place for a mission-station. In one of the streets I met with a Christian young man, who had been schoolmaster at Toomcoor, who rendered me some assistance. After taking an extensive survey of the place, I returned to the first gate, and seeing a large shop, open to the street, unoccupied, I took possession of it, and requested the young man above mentioned to read part of a Canarese tract which he had in his hand. A few people entered the room, but the greater number stood in the street, about two feet below the shop. Novelty brought a congregation of about one hundred, to whom, after the young native man had done reading, I gave a short address on the plan of salvation, and an exhortation to repent and believe in Christ.' When this first little sermon was preached in Goobbe, Daniel and his wife had been living there several years. This day was the commencement of a new era in Daniel's life. Hitherto, from his youth up, though he despised idol worship, he knew nothing about the one true God. Like his neighbours, he believed there were millions of gods, who filled various offices in the government of the world. He had heard of many incarnations of the chief deities, whose good and evil actions are recorded in books held sacred by the Hindoos. He had very confused notions about a future state, but thought there would be a 'judgment' of some kind, followed by rewards and punishments. Also, like all other Hindoos, he was of opinion that when a man dies his soul does not go direct to heaven or to hell, but that it passes into some other body: it may be the body of a human being, or it may be into that of a beast, a bird, a fish, or an insect. And then, after millions of migrations like these, the soul either finds a permanent state of existence according to its fate, or its identity is lost by being absorbed into deity.

Shortly after Daniel heard the first Gospel sermon, Mr. Franklin, an assistant Missionary, was sent by Mr. Hodson from Bangalore to Goobbe, to make certain arrangements for building a mission-house. With him Daniel had long and interesting conversations. He says: 'I was walking one morning with Mr. Franklin outside the town of Goobbe, looking at some land which he thought would be suitable for building a mission-house upon, and, turning, he saw some tombs. He took hold of my hand, and said, "What are those?" I replied, "They are tombs—that is, the place where the dead are buried." He added: "You and I must die and be buried. We shall turn to dust; but there will be a resurrection of the bodies of all men, the raised body will be re-united with its soul, and dwell for ever either in happiness or in misery. The true worshippers of the one true God will go to heaven, and the others to hell. These truths are written in the Christian's *Shastras*. Mr. Hodson and I intend

GOOBEE MISSION COTTAGE,

coming to live at Goobbe, and then we will teach all the people the way to heaven." I was not much impressed with what he said about the Christian Scriptures, but replied, "When Mr. Hodson comes, I hope I shall be employed by him as his washerman?""

## XIII.

### WESLEYAN MISSION COMMENCED AT GOOBBE.

In April, 1837, Mr. and Mrs. Hodson went to live at Goobbe. At first they dwelt in tents, and then they built a little cottage, of which the accompanying sketch gives a fair representation. The walls, about six feet high, were made of mud, the roof was thatch, and the rooms were small and few. But the Missionary and his wife found it very comfortable when the weather was fine, though when it rained they were subject to many little inconveniences. This mission cottage, situated on the brow of a rising ground, commanded a pleasant and extensive prospect. In the front there was a view over hill and dale, wood and water, for fifty or sixty miles. On one side the low flat lands, well watered from a large tank, were covered with rich crops of rice. On other sides there were patches of varied cultivation, interspersed with clumps of trees, as well as large tracts of uncultivated land, used as common pasturage for all the cattle of the town. To these unenclosed grounds cows, sheep, etc., were driven out every morning, and after grazing all day, were brought back into the town of Goobbe every evening. Occasionally, a shepherd's boy, reclining on the ground near his sheep, played sweetly on an instrument, newly made by himself out of some hollow vegetable stalk, but which in an hour or two, on its becoming dry or injured, he would break and throw away as a useless 'bruised reed.' The Missionary has often sat at his cottage door admiring these beauties of nature, when unexpectedly a few graceful timid antelopes have run across the garden in front of him, adding life as well as beauty to the scene. On a Sunday morning he often fancied every thing appeared clearer, brighter and more beautiful than on other days. There was, however, one dark cloud hanging over all this loveliness, in the fact that the town of Goobbe, just at the foot of the hill was wholly given to idolatry;

'Every prospect pleases,
Only man is vile.'

The Missionary and his assistant went forth daily from their poor abodes carrying the riches of the Gospel either into one of the streets of Goobbe, or to some of the numerous villages within seven or eight miles of the mission cottage, and preached in the open air to as many people as they could collect; and when a congregation could not be obtained, they went from house to house, and thus made known the plan of salvation. When they went the first time to any village the people stood in the attitude of attention, but what they heard was so new, that more of wonder than intelligence was manifested by all. After a few visits, when information had increased a little, there was still a manifest disinclination to accept the truth. Because, for a Hindu to be told that in order to salvation he must forsake the idols which his forefathers have worshipped for hundreds of years, and adopt the creed laid down in the *Shastras* of another nation, is to him the height of absurdity. And it very frequently happened that at the conclusion of a sermon the Missionary would hear some one say, 'Very good, all very true; your religion is good for you, and ours is good for us.'

Very few of the people were able to read, so that the distribution of tracts was very limited. They invited all serious enquirers to the cottage to talk about Christianity. Amongst the women who came, some had sickly children with them. On seeing this, Mrs. Hodson administered some simple medicines, which cured several, and their parents attributing the cure to the favour of the Missionary's God, they were for a time very anxious to hear more about Jesus Christ. Reports of these cures were exaggerated, and so mixed up with the New Testament accounts of the miracles performed by Jesus Christ in raising the dead, opening the eyes of the blind, etc., that one poor woman brought her child, who had been blind three years, in hopes that Mrs. Hodson would be able to restore its sight. Amongst the more intelligent visitors was Daniel: and one evening, just after the tent, as a residence, had been abandoned for the thatched cottage, Mrs. Hodson went with her husband to see Daniel's village, Singonahully. No English lady had ever been in the village before, so that there was considerable excitement produced by the visit. Mr. Hodson says, 'As we drew near to the gate of the village we saw two or three boys running to let their parents and others know that the Missionary and his wife were coming. On entering, Daniel showed us his house, and in a very short time nearly all the people of the village, men, women, and children, were gathered together. Having such a large congregation, Mr. Hodson preached a short sermon, but with very little good effect, especially on the minds of the women, for their attention was evidently much more occupied with the shape, colour and material of Mrs. Hodson's dress than with anything her husband said to them.

## XIV.

## VILLAGE WASHERMAN.

DANIEL was by this time regularly installed as Mission Washer*man*. There is no such person as a washer*woman* amongst the Hindoos. Men do the washing in India, and their manner of doing it is very different from the English mode. Instead of using washtubs, etc., etc., as an English washerwoman does, the Indian washerman loads a donkey or two with the dirty clothes, takes them to a tank of good clean water, and there, in the open air, he performs all his purifying operations. Close to the water's edge there is placed a sloping piece of wood, or a large flat stone. The washerman standing close to it, dips the cloth or garment into the water, and taking hold of one end gives the other, which has been dipped, a good swing in the air and brings it down on the wood or stone with a heavy splashing thump. This is repeated again and again, until the cloth or garment is clean. It is then laid out on the grass or rock to dry. In this way Daniel and his relatives had done all the washing required by the farmers and others, in Goobbe and Singonahully, for many years. In their cases ironing or mangling was never thought of. When, therefore, Daniel was sent for to do the Mission-house washing and ironing, he expressed his readiness to do the former, but doubted his ability to perform the latter, and expressed many fears. But Mrs. Hodson shewed him how to wash and also to iron her dresses in the way she wished to have them

WASHERMEN AT WORK.

done. She made him a present of an iron, taught him how to use it, so that, in due time, his work was pronounced satisfactory, and it was acknowledged by all that Daniel stood at the head of his profession—that his skill exceeded that of any other washerman within a circuit of many miles round Goobbe. This little act of kindness in giving the iron to Daniel, was gratefully remembered by him as long as he could remember anything, and he would occasionally shew it to visitors. Under other circumstances he would doubtless have worshipped that smoothing iron as his forefathers did the old swords.

## XV.

## FIRST MISSION HOUSE AT GOOBBE.

MRS. HODSON laid the foundation brick of the Goobbe Mission House on the 24th of May, 1838. The building was finished on the 17th of August following, and cost £180. A few days after it was finished, Mr. and Mrs. John Jenkins, with their child, came to live at Goobbe, and had half the new house (namely, one large room and two small ones) given up to them; the two mission families cheerfully sacrificing a few comforts for the benefit of having an additional preacher in the Circuit. We have seen how Daniel, even when a lad, and without the gospel, treated idols and idolatry; but after the gospel had been preached to him and to his neighbours, the people of his village came round very much to his opinion, greatly to the encouragement of the Missionaries.

## XVI.

### AN ABANDONED HEATHEN TEMPLE.

On the 11th of October, 1839, Mr. Arthur joined Mr. Jenkins at Goobbe, and by that time the fruit of past labour was beginning to appear; not in the shape of individual conversions, but in an extensive neglect of idol worship, particularly in Singonahully. Mr. Arthur gives the following account: 'About the time of my arrival, the inhabitants of the place declared that they had abandoned idolatry, and would no more honour the temple of Runga. To test their sincerity, Mr. Jenkins one morning, asked them whether he might go to the temple. "O, by all means." "Might we enter?" "Yes; go where you like." "Might we enter without taking off our shoes?" "Certainly; we don't care who goes, or how: we have given up the idol." This was strong proof that their old feelings had vanished; and, accordingly, at the temple we found no obstacle to our entrance. Shod and covered, we passed up through the outer apartment to the sanctuary, where sat the grim image of Runga, incrusted in the congealed oil and *ghee* of many anointings, with the lightless lamp before him, faded garlands hanging round his neck, loads of dust settled on his person, and part of the roof falling in directly above. No room remained for doubt. The faith which once adored Runga had changed into contempt; and we rejoiced over that forsaken idol, as an earnest of better days. On afterwards enquiring what induced them to withdraw the confidence they had so long reposed in Runga, they answered, "You (meaning the Missionaries) told us that the god did not protect us, but that we protected the god; that if we only left him alone, we should see that he could not take care of himself; and if he could not take care of himself, how could he take care of us? Now we thought that was a *buddhi matu*, (a word of sense,) and so we resolved to see whether he could take care of himself or not; for we felt certain that if he could not take care of himself, it was out of the question that he could take care of us. Accordingly we discontinued *pooja* (worship). We soon found he could not keep the lamp burning, nor the garlands fresh, nor the temple clean, nor do a single thing for himself. The lamp went out, the flowers withered, the temple became dirty; and then," (they added, laughing) "the roof fell in, just over his head, and there he sat, *soommanay* (tamely) under it; so we saw very well he could not take care of himself." Notwithstanding all this, we had some fears that the return of their annual feast-day would revive their love for heathenish merry-makings with a force too strong for their new convictions. The day came, and we watched the village narrowly. There was no car, no procession, no music: and, when night came, no *tom-tom* was beaten, no rocket sent up, nor any other sign that it was the day of Runga. One morning, when preaching in the village, I observed that the old man who used to con-

IDOL CAST OUT OF SINGONAHULLY TEMPLE.

duct the services of the temple, was not in the congregation; and feeling, for the moment, a suspicion lest he should have returned to his former occupation, I asked, "Where is the *poojari?*" A young man instantly replied, smiling, and patting his person, "O, he has gone to the fields with the cattle: now that the temple is given up, he must do something for his stomach."'

## XVII.

## AN IDOL THROWN OUT OF A TEMPLE.

MR. MALE, who succeeded Mr. Jenkins at Goobbe, has left upon record a further account of what happened to the idol Runga. He says, 'One day in August, 1842, as I was returning from Toomcoor to Goobbe, I overtook a Brahman, and in the course of conversation he enquired whether or not I had heard of what had befallen Singonahully *Runga Swami*. I replied that I had not. He then said, "*Runga Swami* has been thrown out of his temple, and is now outside the door among the stones." "Well," I said, "what do you think will be done?" He answered, "Why, formerly, a great deal of money would have been collected, and with it many things would have been done to purify the god; and then he would have been replaced in the temple; but now the people care nothing about it, no money will be given and nothing will be done. If anything be said to the people of the village on the subject, they will say, "What can we do? We have nothing to give: we did not throw the god out, etc., etc."' Mr. Male adds, 'The remarks of the Brahman were very true, for the people did not do anything to reinstate the idol. I spoke to them several times about the downfall of their god, but they made very light of the matter. However, after the idol had been thus degraded for many weeks, some villagers, out of pity to the poor old priest, promised that they would reinstate the idol when they had money enough to pay for all the ceremonies. The priest, therefore, in order to preserve the idol from further indignities, and also to commence the process of purification, put it into a well near the temple, to remain there, until the villagers performed their promise. The next event, cheering to the Missionaries, was the baptism of Daniel.

## XVIII.

### BAPTISM OF DANIEL.

In the beginning of 1843, the mind of Daniel was brought under a very powerful and gracious influence of the Holy Spirit, which produced an ardent desire for salvation. Hitherto he had been an opponent of idolatry, and he had manifested an interest in the doctrines of Christianity, but he had never shown any deep conviction of his sinfulness and danger, nor any desire to obtain pardon and purity. He had been a diligent hearer of the Word of God, and he had studied its truths well. The Missionaries had established a school in Singonahully, and visited it regularly to examine the boys. At these times many of the parents attended, and took great interest in the progress of their children. Daniel used very frequently to sit in the school listening to the lessons, and, though he was never able to read himself, he had his children taught, and made them read the Scriptures to him day by day for many years. He was blessed with a very retentive memory and with good common sense, so that he had a very fair acquaintance with the history, the biography, and the doctrinal teaching of both the Old and the New Testament. And now, to this knowledge, there was added that special working of the Holy Spirit, which produced deep conviction of sin, and an anxious desire to escape eternal punishment. He says, 'I regularly attended the preaching of the Missionaries, and always felt interested in what they taught, but I did not feel any serious concern for salvation until Mr. Hardey came to live at Goobbe. Under his teaching and prayers I was brought to a better mind; but even then there were some sins which I did not wish to give up. I wanted to save my soul and yet retain some pecuniary advantages connected with heathenism. I and my family had often conversed about our all becoming Christians, and they, every one of them, always declared that they would follow me. This cheered and comforted me. But, for a long time, as often as I decided to go and open my mind to the Missionaries, so often did some strong temptation turn me aside. I feared my uncle who had been very kind to me. And then I thought, all my relations will disown me, and they will unite with other heathens in persecuting me, so that my life will be made miserable. Thus I went on month after month. But at length, in answer to prayer, I received power to decide for Christ and against the world. I went immediately and told Mr. Hardey all that was in my heart. After this, he and Nallamuttoo, the Catechist, daily instructed me and prayed with me for many weeks. I felt the benefit of this teaching, and by Divine aid I was able to say, 'I give up all for Christ.' One day while under this course of instruction, I felt very anxious to be baptized without further delay, and I asked Mr. Hardey to fix upon a day for the baptism. This being done I went home and told my wife and children what I had done: and they all said we will do as you do. Mr. Male was at this time living in Mysore, but as he had known and instructed me before Messrs. Hardey and Sanderson came to live at Goobbe, he was requested by them to come and perform this sacrament of baptism. On his arrival he had a long conversation with me. He asked me many questions, warned me as to coming persecutions, and exhorted me to watchfulness, prayer, and faith. I said, "I believe that in every difficulty God will be my friend and protector. By Divine help, I shall be able to endure: and I am prepared to give up all for Christ.”’

The day fixed for the baptism was Sunday, the 13th of August, 1843; and the place was the Goobbe chapel, near the fort gate, not the present chapel, but the one which was first built in that locality. Out of curiosity many came to see a baptism, and amongst them several of Daniel's relatives. Mr. Male conducted the usual Sunday morning service, and the large congregation was very attentive, both during the sermon and whilst he read a portion of the baptismal service; but when by his movements it became evident to those natives in the congregation who were nearest to him that he was about to make some use of the water, which was in the vessel on a table in front of him, they shrunk back upon the people behind them, and in a moment there was a panic. Some, not knowing exactly how the water would be used, and fearing that a drop or two might by chance fall on them, so as to make them Christians without their consent, rushed to the door; others, in ignorance, followed; and as all tried to get out of the chapel at

BAPTISM OF DANIEL AND HIS FOUR SONS.

once, the doorway was soon blocked up. Then a few men scrambled out at the windows; and in the scuffle two or three children were knocked down, but no one was seriously hurt. The confusion and noise put a stop to the sacred service for several minutes. But when all the congregation had gone out except Daniel and his four sons, Mr. Male proceeded with the service without further interruption. The people who had escaped out of the chapel remained near to it in the street until the service was over. A few peeped in at the open door and windows to gratify their curiosity. The father was named Daniel, and his four sons were named respectively John, Peter, Timothy, Samuel. There were some hindrances in the way of Daniel's wife being baptized with her husband and children; but as Mr. Male happened to be passing through Goobbe six months afterwards, he baptized her then, giving her the name of Sarah, as previously fixed upon. After the baptism of Daniel and Sarah they continued to live in the village of Singonahully, without any serious persecution from their heathen neighbours. This may, perhaps, be accounted for on the ground that the villagers having no love for idolatry, generally approved of Daniel's conduct in embracing Christianity.

## XIX.

### DANIEL AND THE VILLAGE PRIEST.

AFTER his baptism Daniel was very consistent in his conduct as a Christian, and in a quiet way attempted to promote the spiritual well-being of his neighbours. He was well qualified by his knowledge of the Scriptures to set forth the truth as it is in Jesus; and was 'ready always to give an answer to every man that asked him a reason of the hope that was in him with meekness and fear;' and his word was often accompanied with divine power. He had long disputations with the village priest (a nephew of the man who was priest when the idol was thrown out of the temple). His case is a very interesting one. He was a sincere enquirer, and became a regular attendant at Daniel's family prayer. He said one day to the Missionary, 'Although I have walked daily several miles to gather flowers after bathing and putting on my temple garments; although I have gone into the temple and made offerings to the idol; although I have done all this in sincerity to the present time—this idol, neither in my dreams nor when awake, has ever said, "Thy sins are forgiven thee." Although from fear lest the idol should destroy me, I have fasted and prayed, it never said to me, "Thou shalt escape hell and enjoy heaven." Therefore the idol is a lie, and I forsake it. I embrace Jesus Christ as my Saviour and my God.' Mr. Walker gives the following account of him:—

'A few days ago, just as I was leaving the village of Singonahully, after preaching, I saw the *poojari* with his guitar in his hand, going off to another village to beg his bread for the day. I stopped him, and we entered into conversation on the sin of idol-worship. I told him that in order to salvation it was absolutely necessary for him to abandon his idols and embrace Christ as his only and present Saviour. He tried to appear unconcerned, and said, "It is getting late; I must go for alms," and left me. In a few days he came to the Goobbe Chapel, and after the sermon I spoke pointedly to him, asking him, in the presence of the whole congregation, if he was desirous of obtaining salvation. He said, "I am." I asked if his idols could save him. He answered, "No." I then said, "If you will, with all your heart, believe in Christ and become His disciple, He will save you." Throughout this conversation all the people looked at him in amazement. After a few days I went again to Singonahully, and saw the *poojari* in company with Daniel. I preached to a small congregation from a part of the eighth chapter of St. Matthew's Gospel; and in my sermon I proved the divinity of our Lord Jesus Christ from the miraculous cure he wrought upon the leper. I showed to them the leprosy of sin; and after dwelling upon the awful consequences of sin, I exhorted the people to seek for the healing of their spiritual maladies by faith in Jesus Christ. This done, the *poojari* and Daniel accompanied me to my house. At Daniel's request I read the parable of the Pharisee and Publican, and commented on it. The next morning the *poojari* came to my house again, and said he wished to be baptized. I exhorted him to stand steadfast, by faith in Christ, and then prayed with him. He appeared to be deeply affected. He came with Daniel to our next Class-meeting, and joined heartily in our devotions. In a day or two he came to my house again, and gave me the idol which he and his family had worshipped for many years.' He then went home, and told his wife what he had done with the idol, and that he had made up his mind to become a Christian. His wife on hearing this began to beat her breast and cry bitterly. She threatened to go to the mission-house, pull out her tongue and die there. The heathen people in Singonahully, hearing that the priest had given Mr. Walker the idol which he and his family had worshipped, became alarmed, and secured the keys of a temple inside the village, where the priest officiated daily, lest the idol in it should also be taken and given to the Missionary. After a few days the priest's wife ceased her opposition, and began herself to converse with Daniel's wife and others about the truths of Christianity. The villagers annoyed the priest in every possible way. As he could not remain peaceably in his own house, he left the village, and the Missionary gave him a room on the mission premises. Sunday, December 20th, 1846, was the day fixed on for the baptism. The place was the chapel in which Daniel had been baptized about three years previously. The congregation was unusually large, and a solemn awe rested upon the people. The interest increased as the service proceeded. *Vysha Runga* was the priest's heathen name. After he had answered all the questions proposed to him in the presence of the congregation, he was baptized in the name of the Father, the Son, and the Holy Ghost, and was henceforth known by the name of Abraham. On the same day he voluntarily took food with the other Christians, as a public announcement that he had broken his caste. The Missionaries considered that Daniel was the chief instrument, in the hands of God, of this man's conversion.

## XX.

### DANIEL 'MADE A MARRIAGE FOR HIS SON.'

In the year 1848 Daniel 'made a marriage for his son,' and the Missionaries fearing that he might go to some excess either in expenditure or in some worldly conformity, gave him special warning, and watched over the preparations with anxious care. On the wedding day a great number of the friends of both families assembled, and amongst them were many heathens. There were present some who at one time had manifested the greatest hostility to Daniel on account of his baptism. They had refused him access to their houses, and invoked the most dreadful calamities upon him and his family for renouncing the religion of his fathers. However, in many things Daniel had prospered: the blessing of God upon his diligence had placed him in better circumstances than he was in when he embraced Christianity. There was a cheerful generosity in his manner which was well calculated to remove unpleasant feelings, whilst respect was gained by his consistent Christian deportment. This was an illustration of the proverb, 'When a man's ways please the Lord he maketh even his enemies to be at peace with him.' After the marriage ceremony was over, all went together to Daniel's house, which was not large enough to contain half of them. But he had, as is usual on festive occasions, erected a temporary covering at the front part of the house, which was very cool and pleasant. Here at eight o'clock in the evening the marriage supper commenced, and without a drawback of any kind all went on very pleasantly. But the Missionaries felt anxious lest there should be, through mistaken kindness, a yielding in some degree to the customs followed at heathen weddings. They therefore determined to go from the mission-house to Singonahully, so as to arrive about the time when the supper is over, and heathens, on such occasions, commence their music, dancing, etc. They thought that if any ill-advised arrangements had been contemplated they would thus be averted; and also that their presence would be a mark of interest felt in the happiness of the newly-married pair. The delight of the Missionaries may be imagined when, as they approached the house, they not only found all to be peace and good order, but what was more gratifying, the bridegroom was reading a chapter of the New Testament, and Daniel was commenting, at proper intervals, upon what was read, endeavouring to explain and apply the words. The Missionaries sat down in the temporary verandah, where they spent a happy half-hour with the wedding party in religious conversation and prayer. Daniel was full of joy. This was his 'family prayer' on a larger scale than usual. He said to all present, with gratitude to God, 'When I became a Christian, my neighbours told me that I should never be able to get my children married, nor even to procure bread for my family. But God has supplied all my wants. Whatever I have needed He has given, and I have no fears as to the future.' The Missionaries returned home truly thankful to God for this instance of His preserving grace.

## XXI.

## THE GOOBBE CIRCUIT GIVEN UP.

UP to this time Daniel had been sustained by Divine power against all the opposition of his *enemies*. He had been tried and found faithful. But now he had to endure trial from the conduct of his best friends—the Missionaries and the Missionary Committee. In the year 1851, the Society was in debt to a large amount, so that retrenchment was resorted to, and the Mysore District was one of the sufferers. In this difficulty the District Meeting decided to abandon the Goobbe Circuit.

In accordance with this decision, not only were the Missionaries removed, but the Goobbe mission-house, the Goobbe chapel, in which Daniel had been baptized, the school-rooms, and all other buildings, were sold. When the idol was tumbled out of the temple, *Christianity* triumphed; and when the house of God was sold, *heathenism* triumphed. That was not only a bitter day to good old Daniel, but *a terrible blow to the cause of Christ in Goobbe.* Enquirers after the way of salvation enquired no more. Some who had taken a few steps in the narrow path turned back, and never entered it again; while every heathen priest found in this breaking up of the Mission a powerful argument to keep his disciples out of the way to heaven. Whenever Daniel went from his own village to Goobbe, he was derided by the heathen, as Pilgrim was at Vanity Fair. The blasphemy and ridicule with which he was assailed were almost unbearable. One day especially he was most severely tried. As he was going along one of the principal streets some of the 'lewd fellows of the baser sort' were most insulting and abusive; and a few shopkeepers joined them in ridiculing the Christian. His own account is this:

'Some said, "What! did your Missionaries leave Goobbe because they had no food?" "They had nothing to eat, so they sold the bungalow, and the schools, and even God's house! Such is your fate. Have they given *you* any of the money to live upon?" I replied, "God will not forsake me. When I was an enemy to God, He protected and took care of me; and now I am His child, will He forsake me? Never!" They said, "Will your God maintain you if you sit doing nothing at home?" I answered, "It is idleness to sit quietly at home. God has given me strength and a mind to work for my living." One said, "You spoiled your caste when you had every comfort; you are mad." One man, without attempting to ridicule, said solemnly, "All that has happened to him was his fate; it was written in his forehead; let him alone."'

Of course Daniel was much distressed. He went home quite cast down, and in tears told his wife how the people had ridiculed him, and how dejected he felt. But she comforted him by saying—'We are called to bear all these reproaches for Christ's sake, and He will support us under them; He will never forsake us.' At night he had a portion of God's Word read to him as usual, and at family prayer he was much comforted: his faith and hope were strengthened. In this way he went on for four or five years, without any human help except an occasional visit from a Missionary, who, on a preaching tour, turned aside to spend a few hours with him. Daniel says, 'One day the Revs. Messrs. Sanderson and Hardey called to see us, and I exclaimed, "O, Sirs, we are left here as sheep without a shepherd. You have planted a young tree, but it is dying for want of water. The people reproach us, saying, "Your Missionaries having no food, have sold the mission-house, the schools, and even the house of God."' Messrs. Sanderson and Hardey did and said all they could to comfort and encourage the few forsaken Christians, and their effort was not in vain.

## XXII.

## THE GOOBBE CIRCUIT RE-COMMENCED.

In the course of three or four years there was an improvement in the pecuniary circumstances of the Missionary Society, and arrange-

GOOBBE CHAPEL.

ments were made for recruiting the Mysore District. In connection with these changes, Mr. Hodson returned to India. He landed at Madras January 1st, 1854. After being detained there several months, he went to live at Bangalore, and paid his first visit to Goobbe on the 16th of April, 1855. He found the old mission-house in a very dilapidated state. It had become the property of Government, and was used as a travellers' bungalow—a public rest-house for every traveller passing that way who needed accommodation. Mr. Hodson and Daniel soon had an interview, and the past days of trial were brought under review. In the midst of all difficulties and persecutions Daniel had 'kept the faith.' In his conversation with Mr. Hodson, he referred to the time when the first sermon was preached in Goobbe, his being employed by Mrs. Hodson, his conviction of sin, and his baptism. He stated with wonderful correctness many events that had happened in the Mission from its commencement to that day; and some of them were referred to with deep feeling. When Mr. Hodson said, 'We will try to re-purchase this house, build a new chapel, and put a Missionary to live at Goobbe again,'—the good man wept with joy. He said that this revival of the Mission had been his prayer and hope ever since the Missionaries went away. The Government re-sold the mission-house to Mr. Hodson for the sum they had paid the Mission for it. Under Mr. Sullivan's care the house was put into complete repair, and a good substantial chapel was built in the town of Goobbe. Mr. Hodson preached the opening sermon, June 12th, 1860.

## XXIII.

## A CONVERTED VILLAGE BLACKSMITH.

We have already seen how Daniel tried to bring his heathen neighbours into the way to heaven; but another instance of his successful efforts is given by Mr. Sullivan, the then resident Missionary: 'Runga was a blacksmith, a very immoral man, who lived in Singonahully. Daniel instructed him and warned him. He told him of heaven and hell; showed him that unless he repented and believed in Christ he could not be saved. Sometimes Runga was attentive, and his case seemed hopeful, but at other times it was quite the reverse. At length he yielded to Daniel's invitation, and attended morning and evening in Daniel's house at the time for family devotions. After that he began to attend divine service in the Singonahully chapel. He was ridiculed and persecuted by the heathen, but he held on his way. These means of grace were blessed to him. He became penitent, and brought forth the fruits of repentance. The reformation in his conduct was evident to all who observed him. From being a drunkard he became a sober man; and he resolved never to take another drop of intoxicating liquor—a resolution which he faithfully kept to the day of his death. He also became industrious, so that his wife and children, who had formerly been half starved, and who were covered with rags and dirt, now experienced a wonderful change. They had abundance of good food, were well clothed, and their house, as well as their persons, was always neat and clean. But Daniel, though pleased with this outward reformation, was not satisfied; he knew that something more was necessary. He persevered in exhortation and prayer for the man's conversion to God; and he wished him to make an open confession of his faith by baptism. As often as Daniel pressed this duty upon him, so often did Runga declare, 'I am not worthy to be called a Christian; I am not worthy to be as you are. I believe in Christ for salvation, but I am too vile to be honoured with baptism.' One day, by way of showing that he had done with idolatry, he took a number of iron things—not idols, but instruments that had been used in idolatrous ceremonies by himself and his forefathers—and with his own hands he made them into reaping-hooks and other useful farming instruments, preceding his work by the declaration, 'These things won't be wanted any more in their present shape, so I will make something useful of them.' When he was attacked by a fatal disease, some of the villagers said to him exultingly, 'Ah! you have become a Christian; you trust in the Christian's God; let us see if He will cure you; He cannot; our god will kill you.' Daniel said to the sick man, 'Do you believe that their god can harm you?' He said, 'No, no!' Daniel's wife then added, 'But we all think you will die; are you afraid to die?' He answered, 'I am

SINGONAHULLY CHAPEL AND VILLAGE GATEWAY.

not afraid; I believe in the Lord Jesus Christ.' When he became worse, and it was evident that he had not many minutes to live, Daniel said to him, 'Runga, continue to trust in the Lord Jesus Christ.' He replied, 'I believe ONLY on the Lord Jesus Christ,' and in a few minutes he died. He was never baptised, but doubtless he was saved through the merit of Jesu's death, and Daniel was the chief instrument in his conversion.

## XXIV.

### NEW VILLAGE CHAPEL.

UP to the year 1864, one building in Singonahully, had served the double purpose of chapel and school-room. This was not according to Daniel's wish. He thought there ought to be two buildings. And he resolved to erect a school-room at his own expense, and give it to the Mission, as a thank-offering to the Lord for a good harvest; for by this time he was a farmer as well as a washerman. Full of this idea he came to the Mission-house, and with great modesty spoke of the plan which he had made. The Missionary approved of having two buildings, but suggested that instead of building a school-room, it would be better to keep the present building for school purposes, and erect a new chapel. The sum which Daniel had set apart was £4, but this would not build a chapel. However, the Missionary proposed that Daniel should give his £4, and that a few friends should be asked to make up the deficiency. This was done, and the chapel was built. Four pounds may, to some persons, seem a small sum, but He who 'searches the heart,' and Who approved of the widow's two mites, rightly estimated the value of old Daniel's gift; and the Missionary Society would have a larger income than it now has, if all Christians would give the same proportion of their income as Daniel gave on this occasion.

## XXV.

## DANIEL'S SICKNESS AND HAPPY DEATH.

When Daniel was over seventy years of age, he said to a friend, 'It has pleased God to take my wife to himself, and I am now an aged pilgrim near my journey's end. I have been spared to see my children's children, even to the third generation. I have five sons, twelve grandchildren, and eight great-grandchildren. I commit them all to the hand of the great God whom I serve. I pray that He will bless them, keep them all in the way to Heaven, and that I may meet them all in glory. May He help me to wait patiently here until He shall call me into Heaven through the merit of my Lord and Saviour Jesus Christ. God bless the Missionaries and the Mission work abundantly.'

About twelve months before his death, Daniel caused the following testimony to be written, 'I was born in sin, and I lived in the practice of all kinds of iniquity. I performed the ceremonies and followed the customs of our people for many years, but I found no peace in them. Then I began to think about worshipping the *one* God, of whom I had heard something, but I was very ignorant and knew not how to worship Him. While I was thinking much on this subject, the Missionaries came and preached the Gospel. I heard the truth; and by their teaching I was made to understand the way of salvation. I believed on the Lord Jesus Christ with my whole heart, and then I felt that God, for the sake of Christ's merit, had pardoned all my sins. Peace and joy sprung up in my heart: and I now pray for His help to keep me from sin as long as I live. I am nearly eighty years old; my days are uncertain; I do not know when I may die. I have no delight in this world, and I hope to enter the world of glory, through the merit of the death of Christ.'

He became gradually more and more feeble, and for many weeks before he died was blind and nearly deaf. Mr. Haigh, who was then at Goobbe, gives the following account: 'On Saturday evening I went with Mr. and Mrs. Hocken to see Daniel. We found him sleeping on a mattress. He awoke soon after we entered his room, but the attendants found it difficult to make him understand who we were. He did not answer our questions, but muttered a few short sentences, and then after a long pause, he said distinctly, "O, Jesus, take me to Thyself, take me to Thyself." When, at length, his son made him understand who we were, the good old man wept, and said, "Alas! I cannot see them." At this moment of clearer consciousness, his son, at Mr. Hocken's request, asked him if he had joy in thinking of Jesus. He replied, "Yes, great joy."'

Mr. Hocken has given the following account: 'On Saturday evening, October 25th, Mr. Haigh, Mrs. Hocken and myself went from the Mission-house to see old Daniel. We found him lying on a mat, and covered with a white cloth. He appeared unconscious of our presence, and murmured as one in a dream, "Jesu, Swamy, (Lord,) take me to Thy feet." It was some time before he could understand who we were, and then he cried because he could not see us. The villagers crowded round the door, and watched us with almost deathly silence. I tried to draw the old man into conversation, but his mind wandered. At intervals he prayed fervently to Jesus, lingering over, and repeating many times, the name of Jesus. His mind seemed to be continually running on the thought that he should soon be with Jesus. We prayed, and made preparations for giving him the Lord's Supper. As soon as I put the sacramental bread into his hand, a flash of devout joy lighted up his face, and he lifted the bread reverently to his mouth. It was a very affecting sight to see this worthy old Christian taking the Sacrament for the last time. All his family were deeply moved. When we took leave of him he started as he took my wife's hand. He said, "This is a little one, whose is it?" They told him it was Mrs. Hocken's. The old man bent over it and blessed her.'

A few days after this, while the Missionaries were away from Goobbe, Daniel died; and the Catechist gives the following account: 'On the day of his death he appeared to be much better; his hearing and his sight were both partially restored. He could see anyone moving about the room. In the morning, being conscious that he was dying, he asked that all his people might come around him, and when they had assembled he exhorted them all to follow him to heaven. He said, "Give my salam to the Missionaries, and tell them I die happy; my heart is full of love to God." "And when he had said this, he fell asleep."'

HAYMAN BROTHERS AND LILLY, HATTON HOUSE, FARRINGDON ROAD, E.C.